Francis of Assisi

WOLF TAMER OF THE MIDDLE AGES

2019 First printing

Francis of Assisi: Wolf Tamer of the Middle Ages

English translation copyright © 2019 by Paraclete Press, Inc.

ISBN 978-1-64060-207-6

Original French Edition *François d'Assise: Dresseur de loup au Moyen Âge*, © Fleurus Mame—Paris, 2017

The Paraclete Press name and logo (dove on cross) are trademarks of Paraclete Press, Inc.

Library of Congress Cataloging-in-Publication Data is available.

10 9 8 7 6 5 4 3 2 1

Published by Paraclete Press
Brewster, Massachusetts
www.paracletepress.com

Printed in Spain by Edelvives

DELPHINE PASTEAU   ILLUSTRATED BY VIOLAINE COSTA

Francis of Assisi

WOLF TAMER OF THE MIDDLE AGES

San Damiano Books

PARACLETE PRESS

Brewster, Massachusetts

EPISODE

I

1182

In a beautiful home in the city of Assisi, Peter Bernardone, a rich clothing merchant, and his wife, Lady Pica, marvel at their newborn son.

"We'll call him Francis!" exclaims Peter. "In honor of France, the country that made me rich!"

1202

Francis is 20 years old. He is rich, handsome, intelligent, full of joy, and courageous. With his friends, he goes off to war against the city of Perugia, the sworn enemy of Assisi.

"Let's have a toast, my friends! Victory to Assisi!"

A few weeks later, the battle rages at Collestrada. But it is a crushing defeat for Assisi. Francis is taken prisoner.

Francis gets out of prison. He dreams of military glory. His most cherished desire? To become a knight in the armies of the pope.

Upon returning to Assisi, Francis buys himself a beautiful suit of armor, tries it on, and, very proud, parades in the city on his new horse. But his glance crosses with that of Fabio. A ruined noble, Fabio is wearing a shabby suit of armor and is mounted on an old, knock-kneed horse. Immediately, Francis gives Fabio his horse and his armor.

But Francis doesn't stop his project for anything! He leaves for southern Italy to put his sword to work in the service of the pope. On the way, God calls out to him:

"Why serve the servant rather than the master?"

"What do you want me to do, Lord?" asks Francis.

"Return to your country!"

Francis returns to Assisi, feeling distraught. Parties, luxury, money: all of his former life seems to him to be meaningless. From this point on, he wants to serve Christ and Lady Poverty!

To start, Francis gives his money to the poor.
Then, he tries to serve the lepers, whom he has always found repulsive. He takes a first step by giving a coin to a leper. He takes a second step by kissing his hand. Finally, he looks at all lepers, gives them alms, embraces them, and serves them.

Then he leaves on pilgrimage to Rome. Arriving at Saint Peter's Basilica, Francis exchanges his clothing with that of some poor people and tosses his gold on the altar. And then he begins to beg in the streets along with the beggars.

Upon returning to Assisi, Francis goes down to the lower part of the city and goes to the little chapel of San Damiano. It is dilapidated, but Francis likes to come and pray there. On his knees before the wooden crucifix, Francis asks:

"What can I do for you, Lord?"

"Francis, my house is falling into ruins and is falling apart. Go and rebuild it."
The Christ on the crucifix came back to life and answered him!

Francis goes to work. He goes to the markets and sells all of his father's supplies of cloth. With the money he repairs the chapel of San Damiano, and the churches of the Portiuncula and of Saint Peter.

"Well, Lord, Bernardone, your son has become a real tramp! He is hardly dressed, he lives by himself, and he sells your cloth in order to throw money out the window!" This time, it's too much! Peter Bernardone is furious. His son has been making a mockery of him for months. The whole city is making fun of him.

He seizes Francis and drags him to a square. In front of the crowd and Guido, the bishop, he shouts:

"I am disinheriting you! You are no longer anything to me. Get out of this city!" Francis takes off his clothes and declares:

"In complete freedom, from now on I will be able to say, 'Our Father who is in heaven!' Peter Bernardone is no longer my father. I give him back his money and all my clothes. I will go naked to meet the Lord."

At these words, the bishop covers Francis with his cloak.

1209

Francis lives near the Portiuncula with some companions.

"My friends, in listening to the Gospel yesterday, I understood that the Lord was sending us on a mission. We must give everything for the poor."

Soon, other men renounce their worldly goods in order to follow Francis's rule of poverty: Bernard, Giles, Peter. Francis sends them to preach two by two. The Franciscans are born.

1212

In turn, Clare, a young noble woman, gives up everything and, following Francis's model, founds an order of women religious: the Poor Clares.

One day, Francis sees a large number of birds in a thicket. He tells them,
    "Dear brother birds, praise the Lord for his graces: your beautiful feathers, your colors. The Lord takes care of you."
At these words, the birds flap their wings and chirp joyfully. Francis blesses them, and they all take flight.

Francis's road passes next through Gubbio. Francis meets a wolf that is terrorizing the population of that little village. He then traces a sign of the cross over it and tells it,
    "Brother Wolf, in the name of Christ, I command you no longer to hurt anyone."
The wolf nods in agreement. He then becomes the friend of the inhabitants of Gubbio, who give him food to eat.

1219

The Fifth Crusade has lasted for almost two years. The Crusaders want to free Christ's tomb in Jerusalem. They pass through Egypt. After the battle, thousands of dead lie near Damietta, on the Nile delta. A truce is established between the Crusaders and the Muslims.

Francis takes advantage of the truce to cross the enemy lines. With a companion, Brother Illuminatus, they go to see the sultan, Malek al-Kamil. The sultan receives them with great courtesy. Despite the friendship that develops between the men, Francis does not obtain the peace he hopes for. He finishes the Crusade in prayer and in pilgrimage.

1223

"Brothers, at the approach of Christmas, look at all these Christians who leave our churches to go to Bethlehem. This is a very dangerous pilgrimage. And those who remain behind no longer have a great desire to celebrate the birth of our Savior. We need to bring this celebration more alive!"

"How do we do that?" asks Bernard.

"We are going to recreate a manger scene for the Christmas Mass, as in Jesus's time!" No sooner said, then done! Francis chooses a cave in Greccio. He brings an ox and a donkey, and he prepares a manger to serve as the altar. All the people of the surrounding villages come with torches and candles. Songs echo through the forest. What a beautiful Christmas celebration!

1224

Francis prays more and more. He desires ever more greatly to be close to the Lord. Suddenly, Francis sees holes in his hands and in his feet. Blood flows out of them. These are the same wounds as those of Jesus on the cross: Francis has just received the stigmata.

Francis's last years are hard. He is sick and almost blind. But he writes the canticle of the creatures:

"Blessed are you, Lord, for Sir Brother Sun, Brother Wind, Sister Water, and our mother the Earth."

1226

Francis dies on the ground in the little church of the Portiuncula.
He is proclaimed a saint only two years after his death.
The Franciscans, who numbered only 12 at the start, are 5,000 at the end of Francis's life, and 35,000 today.

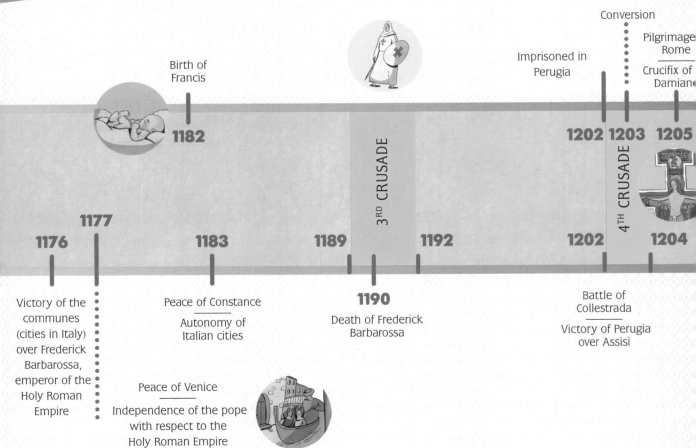

Birth of Francis

1182

3RD CRUSADE

Imprisoned in Perugia

1202

Conversion

Pilgrimage Rome

Crucifix of Damiano

1203

1205

4TH CRUSADE

1176

1177

1183

1189

1192

1202

1204

Victory of the communes (cities in Italy) over Frederick Barbarossa, emperor of the Holy Roman Empire

Peace of Constance
___
Autonomy of Italian cities

1190

Death of Frederick Barbarossa

Battle of Collestrada
___
Victory of Perugia over Assisi

Peace of Venice
___
Independence of the pope with respect to the Holy Roman Empire

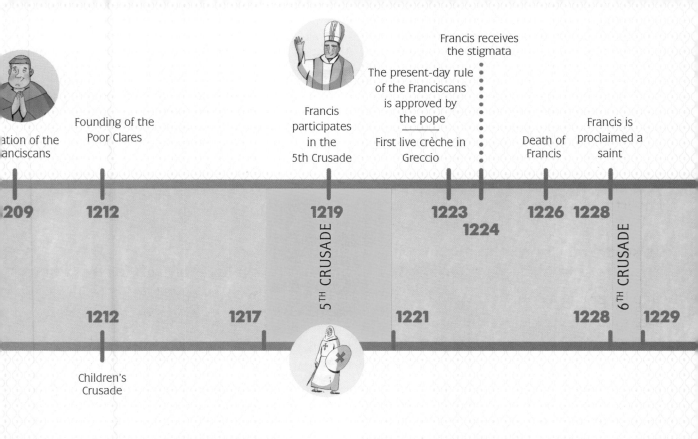

ation of the
anciscans

Founding of the
Poor Clares

Francis
participates
in the
5th Crusade

The present-day rule
of the Franciscans
is approved by
the pope

First live crèche in
Greccio

Francis receives
the stigmata

Death of
Francis

Francis is
proclaimed a
saint

209 1212 1219 1223 1226 1228
1224

5TH CRUSADE

6TH CRUSADE

1212 1217 1221 1228 1229

Children's
Crusade

And during this time, in the medieval world...

THE CRUSADES

The Crusades were **military and religious expeditions** organized by the pope **to free the tomb of Christ in Jerusalem.**

The Christians tried to retake the city of Jerusalem, which had been in the hands of the Muslims since the 7th century. Until the 11th century, Christians could still go to Jerusalem on pilgrimage. But in 1071 the Turks took the city and forbade Christians from going to pray there. In **1095**, at **Clermont-Ferrand**, Pope **Urban II** called for Christians to retake the tomb of Christ and to protect the Christians of the East. Nine Crusades took place between 1096 and 1271. Peasants, knights, and even kings participated in them. The Crusaders took Jerusalem in 1099. But the city was retaken by Muslims one hundred years later. The Fifth Crusade, in which Saint Francis participated, was a failure. The Crusaders were able to retake Jerusalem only at the end of the **Sixth Crusade in 1229.**

▼ **The crusade routes**

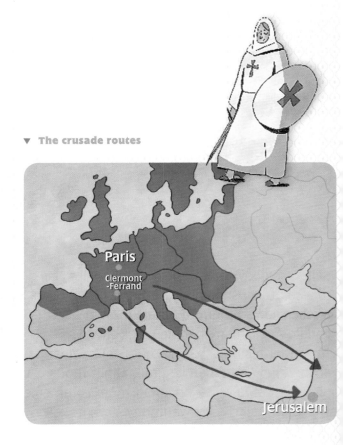

The religious

The artisans

The nobles

The peasants

The clergy

DO YOU KNOW?

Medieval Society
Medieval society was divided into three orders:
– The clergy (the priests and the religious). They prayed for everyone.
– The nobles (the lords and the knights). They fought in order to protect others.
– The peasants, the artisans, and the merchants. They worked and paid taxes to feed the priests and the knights.

IN SEARCH OF RELICS!
Relics are body parts or objects that belonged to a saint. Christians believed that to pray near a relic allowed them to obtain **miracles**. In the Middle Ages, many people went on **pilgrimage**. To attract pilgrims, having relics was a clear advantage. And when you talk about more pilgrims, you are talking about more commerce! This is why each city wanted to have its relics, going so far as trafficking in them, even stealing relics!

Since Francis was proclaimed a saint only two years after his death, his body was the object of envy. So, the city of Perugia would have loved to steal the relics of Saint Francis from their rival, Assisi. Without success! All the inhabitants of Assisi watched over these precious relics day and night.

7 Differences

Find the 7 differences between the two Francises

Follow the trail of Francis

It's Christmas night in Greccio. You must cross the forest to arrive at the cave in which the first live crèche was held. Leaving the forest at the bottom, you must first take a lantern, then go in search of all the animals before meeting up with the crèche.   Watch out! Don't fall into the holes!

Investigate

The day after Saint Francis's death, Brother Bernard opens the gate of the Portiuncula. Dozens of animals come out of the chapel and position themselves as if they want to say something important...

No doubt it's a message transmitted by Francis...

Decode this secret message:

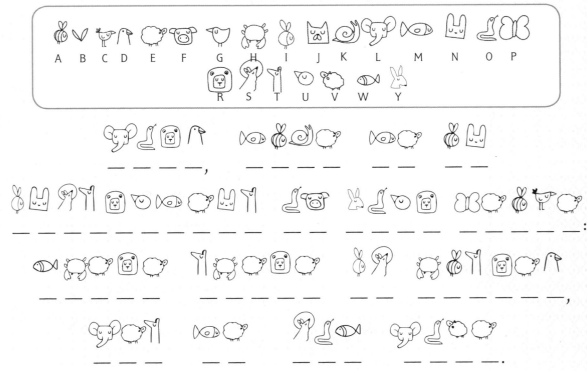

QUIZ

1. In what historical period does this story take place?
a. Modern times
b. Antiquity
c. The Middle Ages

2. Which city was the rival of Assisi?
a. Pisa
b. Perugia
c. Florence

3. Who was Francis?
a. The son of a merchant
b. The son of a peasant
c. The son of a noble

4. What was the sickness suffered by the first sick people that Francis went to serve?
a. The plague
b. Leprosy
c. Cholera

5. In Episode IV, who spoke to Francis?
a. The Virgin Mary
b. Saint Joseph
c. Jesus Christ

6. Who was Francis's first companion?
a. Bernard
b. Peter
c. Giles

7. Which saint founded the female branch of the Franciscans?
a. Clotilde
b. Caroline
c. Clare

8. To which animals did Saint Francis preach a sermon?
a. Wolves
b. Birds
c. Rabbits

9. In which Crusade did Francis intervene?
a. The Second Crusade
b. The Fourth Crusade
c. The Fifth Crusade

10. At the end of his life, what did Francis receive?
a. The first crèche
b. The canticle of the creatures
c. The stigmata

SOLUTIONS

7 Differences

Follow the trail

Investigate

Francis's secret message is:

Lord, make me an instrument of your peace: where there is hatred, let me sow love.

Quiz

Answers: 1-c ; 2-b ; 3-a ; 4-b ; 5-c ; 6-a ; 7-c ; 8-b ; 9-c ; 10-c.

10/10	**8 to 9 points**	**6 to 7 points**	**4 to 5 points**	**less than 4 points**
Terrific ! ! !	Very Good !	Were you dreaming a little ?	Hmmm...	Reread the book!